CHRISTMAS MALL FOLLIES

A MAN GOES SHOPPING

Pat Hester

To shop is to drop. This book is for all who have dropped.

"*Shopping is a woman thing. It's a contact sport like football. Women enjoy the scrimmage, the noisy crowds, the danger of being trampled to death, and the ecstasy of the purchase.*"

—ERMA BOMBECK

"*Most guys have about 73 calories of shopping energy, and once these calories are gone, they're gone for the day- if not the week- and can't be regenerated simply by having an Orange Julius at the Food Fair.'.*

—DOUGLAS COUPLAND, *Microserfs*

"*It saddened me that sometimes shopping was far more perilous than dealing with zombies and vampires.'.*

—ANTON STROUT, *Dead Waters*

CHAPTER ONE

Diagnosing My Problem

"You know what your problem is? You don't have "The Christmas Spirit." You need to get out there and put yourself in it."

Put myself in it? Wanting desperately to be lectured further, I encouraged my friend to continue.

"All you do every year is go online and take the easy way out of shopping. You're missing all of the fun!"

This was partially true. For the past three years, I had, indeed, gone online and purchased nearly all of my Christmas gifts. And it was also very easy as my friend had said. But I didn't think I was really missing out on any fun. Did I really need to hear the Muzak version of "Feliz Navidad" while hunting for insane deals?

Also, it seems to me that when a person attempts to include the words "shopping" and "fun" in the same thought, they suffer from one of two afflictions. Either they are 1) The recent victim of a blunt force trauma to the head, Or 2) They lack a thesaurus on their bookshelf. Roget's Thesaurus currently lists several antonyms for the word "fun" including "annoying", "boring", "tiring", and "sad." Any of these would have been a much better word choice for my friend's sentence.

Don't get me wrong. It's not as though I despise shopping. It's just that, I really, really hate it. I've often wondered where this feeling comes from. My conclusion, based on the best science and research of the day is this: I have an aversion to idiots. When a few yahoos get together in a public place, it's mildly annoying. But when you put a few hundred yahoos in a large retail setting, you have a full-blown circus on your hands. And I'm not talking about the fun kind staged by the Ringling Brothers, either.

My low opinion of shopping isn't a recent development. I remember feeling this way even when I was a kid. My mom used to take me to department stores and I waited in agony while she looked at clothes. I even invented games to try and stay engaged. Sometimes, I hid in the clothes racks and made fart sounds to spook the other shoppers. It was a dark time for me.

One caveat: I don't hate all shopping, just the versions of it that I've tried thus far. Not all of them have been properly tested. For example, I've never tried "Doctor Shopping" but I've heard some good things. And one of these days, I'll get around to trying that website that lets you shop for a bride. Who knows? It could be fun. But mostly, my shopping experiences up to this point have been underwhelming.

You may not realize it but this is a dangerous position for me to hold. My dislike of shopping puts me at odds with my very own country. Roughly 70% of the United States economy is composed of personal consumption. I've no idea what makes up the remaining 30%. Maybe pyramid schemes and the mafia? This means that the success of the country depends not only on me buying stuff I need but also buying piles of stuff that I don't need. My displeasure of hanging out in malls probably makes me an official enemy of the state. So there's that good news.

Besides, the online merchants have made it too easy. For a guy like me, just having the ability to buy gifts on the internet is a blessed thing. To be able to do all of it in ten minutes is almost enough to bring me to a holy place of spiritual enlightenment. I now pray every day at my keyboard. Yes, "The Christmas Spirit" is alive and well on the internet.

By the way, I'm not sure but I'm assuming the term "The Christmas Spirit" may have already been purchased, copyrighted, and/or hijacked by a large retail conglomerate or greeting card maker by now. So, every time I reference the phrase in this book, I probably should add a registered trademark to the end of it. At the very least, I should put it around quotes so I don't get sued, or something. Not that I have any money at all to give to them.

And let's make something else clear: Despite my friend's accusation, I know plenty about this thing called "The Christmas Spirit." I had a great teacher. Most of the information I have on the topic comes from television. Some of it good. Some of it bad. A mixed bag, as they say.

Alas, television has taught me lots of great lessons about "The Christmas Spirit." Rudolph taught me that it was O.K. to be different. Charlie Brown showed me that true friendship is invaluable. And when Frosty The Snowman melted under the blazing sun, I knew that global warming wasn't a hoax. All of these were good things for a kid to learn.

What wasn't so good to learn growing up was the existence of a certain day on the holiday calendar. The day still makes me shudder every time I hear its name. The ironic thing is that millions of people worship it as though it were sacred. But make no mistake. The day they label "Black Friday" is sinister and evil.

CHAPTER TWO

The Running Of The Walruses

I've always been fascinated in watching Black Friday. But only from from a distance. I think the spectacle attracts me in the way in which some people are intrigued by burning buildings or train wrecks. The scenes of hysterical crowds on T.V. are hard to look away from. However, because most of my information on Black Friday comes from news reports, I've developed a few false assumptions over the years.

First, the shoppers who participate in Black Friday are not crazed lunatics as the reports imply. Some of them are also rabid. And secondly, Black Friday used to remind me the Running of the Bulls tradition in Pamplona, Spain. This too, I would later find out, was false.

Like Pamplona's bulls, the shoppers on Black Friday cause their fair share of chaos. And like Pamplona, some casual observers of the event itself show genuine fear as the stampeding groups are released. But to me, that's where the comparison ends. What the typical news report doesn't show is what happens after the release. Five minutes after the gate opens, the Black Friday shoppers return to their natural state, as awkward and lumbering sloths. All of the early aggression and attitude is gone. Running of the Bulls? More like the Running of the Walruses.

The reason for this is simple. The diets consumed by American shoppers to prepare for the rigors of Black Friday are actually very similar to the diets they consume on a normal day. Which is to say Milk Duds and Big Gulps. And although bulls have never been given Milk Duds and Big Gulps in captivity, if they had, they would lose important things. Like stamina. And endurance. Oh, and also they would be hideously diabetic. Bulls-1, Black Friday Shoppers-0.

There are other misconceptions. Contrary to popular belief, Black Friday wasn't invented to give shoppers a jump start on the holiday season. It was created to let people experience what a prison riot felt like from the inside. Now, millions of shoppers can take that off of their bucket list.

It is widely known that many people who participate in Black Friday wake up very early in order to get a good spot in line. And as a result, they hope and pray that their forced insomnia was enough to *potentially* save them a little money. This is somewhat ironic. Due to exhaustion, most of these same people will then call in sick to work the following Monday morning. You know, to the same place where they receive *guaranteed* money in the form of a... paycheck.

With so many people shopping at the same time, things like crowd control and security become essential for retail businesses. Thankfully, each store hires exactly one part-time high school student to help. To assist the inexperienced and under qualified worker in preparing, the stores ask them to think of Black Friday as if it were a battle that needs to be won. "Above all, don't let the unruly crowds overwhelm you!', orders the store manager. And so, for the new hires, training manuals feature strategies from battles that displayed effective crowd control in the past. Like Custer's Last Stand. And the Alamo.

Some large department stores choose to stay open for the entire 24 hour cycle. These stores depend heavily on Black Friday sales in order to meet the bottom line. One of the product categories that brings in a lot of money are the perfumes and fragrances. The counter agents spray beautiful smelling scents to lure shoppers into buying more merchandise. Unfortunately, since most Black Friday shoppers don't shower, the only aroma wafting through the store air is a rancid body odor. Eau de toilette has morphed into "Eau de Sweat."

How bad is the smell? On some occasions, when items aren't in stock, shoppers are given something called a "Raincheck." However, on Black Friday, a Raincheck doesn't mean a temporary hold on merchandise. Rather, it signifies that you've been requested by a member of the staff to go outside and stand in the rain for 30 minutes and check your smell. Because, well, you really stink.

In order to participate in Black Friday, you need to have some form of currency to make a transaction. Most shoppers on Black Friday know this because they have shopped on this day many times. They are veterans of the experience. And so, they come armed with seven high-interest credit cards that are close to being maxed out. That is the beauty of credit. "Buy Now, and then Pay Vastly More Later."

Also, people who participate in Black Friday are not humble. They often claim that they experience and feel "The Christmas Spirit" more than the rest of us. And their actions don't lie. After spending $1,000 on a state-of-the-art flat screen T.V. that is larger than most highway billboards, the shopper will go out of his way to flip a nickel in the Salvation Army kettle. Because, you know, giving is its own reward.

If you are a store owner, and want to be successful on Black Friday, you need to be well-versed in sound business principles. Such as the "80-20 Rule" This classic rule states that 80% of all customer injuries occur from 20% of your own store's employees.

I'm proud to say that I maintain a perfect 0-for-40 record in Black Friday appearances. It's a record I intend to keep until the day I die. And I think it's one of the greatest records in all of sports. That is, if you consider elbowing fellow human beings in the ribs at a Wal-Mart on Black Friday a "Sport." And who doesn't? If my streak is ever broken, I intend to quit the game.

Still, my friend's earlier words had me thinking. What if I really *am* missing out on "The Christmas Spirit?" What if my online shopping habits have prevented me from taking in all of the love, warmth, and good cheer that a shopping mall at Christmas has to offer? You only go around this ride once. And I'll be damned if I'm gonna be denied my yearly allowance of "Christmas Spirit." To the mall, I go!

CHAPTER THREE

I Saw It First

A shopping mall at Christmastime is sort of like a monument to Chinese Fire Drills. Everybody is scurrying. And there is little rational thought on display. Some who observe the relentless activity might compare it to ants building an ant hill. But this is grossly unfair to the ants. The ants have a method to their madness. They are preparing shelter and food for their ant friends. Christmas shoppers have but one low purpose: To annoy the ever living hell out of me. And at nowhere on the Christmas mall property do they perform this better than the parking lot.

My experience at the lot should be pretty easy, assuming I bring enough riot gear and pepper spray. What won't be easy is finding a parking space. Unfortunately, parking help at the Christmas mall is hard to find. The Department of Motor Vehicles teaches me nice things like proper driving technique and the importance of treating others like a number. But they offer no instruction on how to find good parking.

And thus, I have to improvise. My previous trips to the mall taught me a lot of important lessons. I've learned that if I'm going into battle, I need a good battle plan. I'm confident that my parking lot playbook will help me land the space of my dreams. Here is the condensed version:

1) LEARN TO SWEAR. It's the native tongue of any Christmas parking lot. As a kid, I once learned three new swear words when my mom yelled at a guy who took "her" space. If you feel your delivery isn't convincing, watch "John McEnroe's Greatest Meltdowns" on YouTube for further instruction.

2) BE REALISTIC. Cars parked within 1,000 yards of the mall entrance will never leave. Ever. I have succumbed to madness trying to disprove this. Forget them and try a different lot in the next county.

3) THINK SMALL. Compact cars have a much better chance of fitting into parking spaces. Unfortunately, my Honda Civic compact is way too big. So I use a smaller vehicle. The car I use for my trip to the mall was formerly driven by a Shriner in a parade.

4) SHOW EMPATHY. Leaving adequate space between car doors is important. But this is often very hard to judge. Instead, I leave my parking lot neighbors some

fun alternatives. Re-entering their car through a sunroof is an option they will appreciate having.

5) DEFEND YOURSELF. Turn signals are my way to claim a parking space. When this fails to convince others, I bring out my secret weapon: Juvenile reasoning. "I saw it first!" is exactly the sort of clever rationale that will hold up in a court of law if acting like adult doesn't work for me.

6) RESPECT THE ELDERLY. If I spot an old grandmother with emphysema who has trouble finding her car, I don't berate her for being slow. That's rude and lacks class. Instead, I loudly honk my horn several times.

7) PLAY FAIR. My great temptation of the Christmas parking lot is to use a handicapped spot and hope nobody sees me. But this is illegal. Handicapped spaces are designated only for people with medical conditions, serious injuries and, possibly, mullets.

8) STAY FOCUSED. Remember what makes up "The Christmas Spirit": Holiday cheer and goodwill toward men. Neither of these ever resulted in rock-star parking for me. Just saying.

9) STEP ON IT. My heavy car lacks good closing speed. And in order to snag a space, I need to be able to speed up quickly and stalk my prey. To go faster, I consider jettisoning some of the heavier items in my car like the spare tire or Aunt Martha.

10) BE HONEST. If someone parks too close to my car, I don't leave a nasty note attached to his wiper blade. He may not notice it. Instead, I write a lengthy manifesto with shaving cream on his windshield. My message will include a reference about how his poor parking skills ruined not only my holiday but probably my entire life up to this point.

As I drive down the row, I see a car leaving its space on the next row over. So, I do what any other rational person would do. I accelerate to a dangerous speed and swerve within inches of pedestrians to snag the space. I put my turn signal on. And I wait patiently. This space is mine.

Only it's not. Incredibly, the car goes back into the space. Apparently they forgot to buy a holiday Chia Pet or whatever the cheap, "Made In China" trinket of the season happens to be. People like this have a special place reserved not in Hell, but rather in Heaven, where God teaches angels what not to do to earn their wings.

After losing that space, I admit defeat and accept the surrender terms of the lot: The abandonment of my car on someone's driveway and walking 5 miles back to the mall. "The Christmas Spirit" is flowing through my veins. As I approach the door to the mall, I try and forget what happened in the lot and move on. Surely what exists inside has to be better than what just happened outside. Surely.

CHAPTER FOUR

How Can I Help You Today?

In a previous chapter, I tried comparing Christmas shoppers in America to walruses. It turns out I was wrong. They actually more closely resemble confused penguins. As I enter the mall's large department store, the first thing I notice isn't the sale going on but rather, the customers' bizarre gait. It can't be described as walking. Or even sauntering. Nope. These people are waddling.

This action creates both a problem and an opportunity for me. When large numbers of shoppers begin to waddle, their lateral shifting is actually more pronounced than any forward progress. So, the clumsy swaying from side-to-side prevents me from passing them in the store's narrow lanes. I've experienced similar movements at many state fairs.

On the other hand, that same lazy strolling draws immediate attention, usually from an annoying salesman. "How can I help you today?!!!!", barks Stan, an over-caffeinated staff member. Normally, I would rely on the cluster of mall waddlers to fall for this question and be lured away by the possibility of big savings. But today they ignore Stan completely and venture into the mall. They are enticed by something greater. Apparently a gourmet gelato stand had just opened up or something.

"What about you? What shirt size are you?!!!" Stan is persistent. As I stand frozen, I think about the consequences of my answer. I used to answer questions like these with a rather meek, "Thanks, I'm just looking." But that's a terrible reply. Why is it bad? Well, to a salesman, that statement actually means, "I'm indecisive. Please proceed to annoy the hell out of me for the duration of my visit."

Additionally, through years of societal refinement and a general sense of political correctness, I can no longer answer with, "It's not that I don't like you. It's just that I don't like talking with you." So, in a panic, I resort to my emergency backup plan. I answer him in Spanish.

"Me gusta pastel de cumpleanos!" This means, "I like birthday cake." And it's the only complete sentence of Spanish I remember from 4 years of instruction. This sentence will repel even the most persistent salesman on the floor. If the salesman repeats his question, then repeat your love for Spanish birthday cake, only louder. Most will give up, shrug their shoulders and move on resulting in a win for you.

I was feeling good about my escape from Stan but I knew that I couldn't pull the same stunt with every salesman in the mall. After all, I still need to buy a shirt for my dad. And at some point I'll need to interact with one of them without pretending to be from Guadalajara. So I venture to a trendy clothing store with the goal of buying that new shirt.

Inside the store, I'm greeted by Lisa, a store employee. Lisa takes the time to ask me a few questions, and I tell her about the shirt I need. I know not all salespeople are annoying and I'm willing to give her every benefit of the doubt. After all, selling isn't easy. It takes a lot of effort on the part of the salesperson. And Lisa is doing her best to make the sale today.

The first thing Lisa does is that she respects my personal space. Giving customer's their personal space is an important way to show that you respect them. But Lisa's idea of personal space is different than mine. I think she is operating by the rule that if you, the seller, are further away than the customer's own shadow, you are too far. Don't be shy!

As I browse the shirts I find one that looks great. But they don't have my dad's size. I ask Lisa if she can check and see if another location might have it. Lisa agrees and marches to the back room. On the surface, I'm glad that I'm receiving such great customer service. In reality though, Lisa has actually gone to the back room, taken out her smartphone, and spent 5 minutes texting her boyfriend about dinner later. When Lisa comes back, she says, "I checked everywhere and we are all out of this one. Sorry!"

Not wanting to lose the sale, Lisa employs a sales tactic to try and build rapport with me. With Christmas sales, if you can make a customer laugh, you create a powerful connection with him. After all, laughter is infectious. However, Lisa laughs at my lame joke about the weather so hard and with such conviction that she begins to snort out of her nose. Yes, laughter is indeed infectious and now I've been infected with the flu by Lisa.

I feel bad for her. She appears to be trying too hard this Christmas. If she really wants to personalize the transaction, an easy way to do this is to remember a customer's first name. Using name recognition exercises, you can create meaningful pathways to remember names. And I show Lisa how it's done. For example, let's say that I'm a customer named Alan and I walk into the store. Alan is bald. An animal that is bald is a bald eagle. Bald Eagles have talons. The word Talon rhymes with

Alan. Congratulations! You've just made the sales process easier. However, when Lisa tries this trick, she can only muster the following, "So, Baldie, have you made a final decision on that shirt?"

Not wanting to spend any more time in the store, I pick up a shirt that my dad probably won't like and that will never fit him and make my way to the register. Making a store transaction at Christmas used to be a fairly simple process. But now shoppers must answer 26 questions before you can walk out the door: "Which associate helped you today?", "Would you like to sign up for our store credit card?", "Do you want your receipt with you or in the bag?", "Can I have your zip-code?", "Credit or debit, today?", "How many sexual partners have you had the past year?". On and on they go. Do any of the questions improve my store experience? Of course not.

My favorite question asked at the register is, "Are you a member of our store rewards program?" Whenever I'm asked this question, I immediately follow-up with, "Can I be a member of your Punishments Program?" The Punishments Program is, of course, something I invented. But if I had my way, it would work something like this: If a salesperson annoys me to the point of me punching him in the face, then the price of my merchandise is increased by 10% at the register. A small price to pay to relieve some holiday aggression.

As I walk out the door, I notice that the woman who rang me up folded the shirt in a very nice and clean way. Good for her. Folding clothing is a great way to show the customer that you care. However, later I discover a weird object attached to the shirt that isn't the price tag but a security tag. Leaving the security tag filled with dye on the same piece of clothing is a great way to show the customer you really don't give a crap.

My experience at the trendy clothing store took a lot out of me. And answering those questions has made me hungry. Maybe I can find something good at the food court.

CHAPTER FIVE

Slurp And Gulp

Although I survived my interaction with Lisa, I need some space. Dealing with Christmas employees who are also on Ritalin often has that effect on me. It's no big deal. I just need a moment alone with my thoughts to regroup. Unfortunately, even my thoughts are against me today. Or rather, a single thought appearing in my mind right now.

The thought on my mind isn't complicated. It's only eight words. But collectively, these words make up the most regrettable sentence I've yet constructed in the English language: "You know what, a corn dog sounds good." The eight word sentence that should be on my mind is, "Walk away now; gas stations serve better food." If I'm looking for "The Christmas Spirit", I don't think it exists here.

It's my firm belief that a shopping mall food court at Christmastime is quite possibly the saddest place on Earth. And I'm not talking about the crying babies who are wailing loudly. This doesn't bother me. The world has about 2 billion crying children at any given time. Today, my food court is hosting half of them. But I don't find this sad.

No, I'm talking about grown adults openly sobbing in public. It seems a few of them have entered the search term, "Hot Dog Ingredients" and have been reading the results on their smartphones. It could be a while until the shock wears off.

Even the fortunes given out at the Chinese food place are depressing. Next to where I'm standing, a mall Santa is on his lunch break, reading a piece of paper in a fortune cookie that says: "A solid bowel movement may be in your future."

The strange thing about the mall food court is that there are no windows. Much like a casino in Las Vegas, the food courts don't want you to know what time of the day it is. If you did, you may discover that you were eating a breakfast burrito at 3:00pm in the afternoon. You may also discover that the same breakfast burrito was actually made four days earlier.

When Christmas shoppers become hungry, all decorum is thrown out the window. They forget even the most basic of manners. Well, that's not entirely true.

Within the food court, it's the only place in the world where slurping is considered an accepted form of greeting. Still, the place is littered with trash. Wrappers are everywhere. The trash cans reached capacity hours ago. Food isn't chewed. It is inhaled. The guy sitting next to me actually eats half of his Styrofoam plate before realizing it's not a part of his burrito. The place looks like it was attacked by a herd of wild hyenas.

I used to feel bad that any human being had to come in after all of this carnage and attempt to clean it up. The dried up ketchup alone would require a professional sand blaster for removal. But then I remember a documentary I once saw on the "World's Most Dangerous Jobs." It turns out that the malls don't hire cleaning crews but rather demolition crews. Every night, after closing, men come in, lay dynamite, and then proceed to blow up the entire food court. After the dust settles, contractors build a new food court. And that process resumes every night. Malls don't do this because they are insane. Malls do this because it is cheaper than hiring an actual cleaning crew.

The average Christmas shopper who arrives at the food court has spent thousands of dollars on merchandise for their family and friends. They are tired from holding bags. Their backs are hunched over. And they are a little delirious. So many of these shoppers decide to treat themselves to something nice in the food court.

But somehow I don't think any of them wanted to treat themselves to adult-onset diabetes.

Anybody can be a chef in a food court. Vast sums of money have been spent by aspiring chefs in order to train and learn how to be a master chef at a fine restaurant. I have come to realize that these chefs have been wasting their money. For, in the food court, the "chefs" have but one duty: to peel off a plastic wrapper that covers food in a tray. Plenty of chefs are making a living doing this one act. This is considered "Cooking" at the food court.

Within the food court, trays are used to keep food items organized. Trays were invented to help you carry your food items back to the table. However, trays were not invented to place five 64 oz. sodas on at the same time. When the woman in front of me attempts to do this, two of her sodas tip over and spill on the already sticky floor. As expected, nobody attempts to clean the mess. They must be out of demolition dynamite.

One of the most important activities of food court etiquette is table saving. At Christmastime, table saving helps you and your party secure space to eat before some other rotten, greedy bastard does. I thought games like these died out in high school but they thrive at the food court. There are 82 tables in my food court. 81 of them are currently in use. The last remaining table is saved by a lone teenager. "The Christmas Spirit" is on full display when he fails to offer the table to an expecting mother with three crying kids. No dice, mom. I guess you've never heard the saying, "First Come, First Served."

The conditions are dirty but I don't feel too sorry for the food court employees. Although most of them stopped receiving a salary after the recession in 2008, they are still compensated rather handsomely. In the form of gift certificates. To the other food court places. That is why you occasionally hear that classic holiday expression: "Every time a cash register rings, a food court employee gets his Buffalo Wings."

After settling in my chair, I open the wrapper and discover the pimple-faced worker got my order wrong. What I ordered was a corn dog. What they gave me is a bag of fish sticks. I'm reminded of the sacred Bible verse: "Give a man a fish and he eats for a day. Teach a man to order fish sticks from a food court, and he will occupy a spot on a toilet for a lifetime." But I'm too tired to complain. If I did complain, the workers may have spit twice on my recovered corn dog instead of only once on my fish sticks, which is the industry standard. You see, one must make sacrifices at the Christmas food court.

And besides, the line is too long. So, I make the most of it and decide that the "re-processed, artificial fish product in the form of a shape not encountered in any natural setting that is on my plate" will be my supper. I'm hoping it isn't my last supper.

I've heard that some psychologists urge patients experiencing stress to picture calm or serene settings in their minds in order to endure a trying ordeal. But I'm not sure any image I could conjure will be enough to counter the stench of the secret sauce on these holiday fish sticks. I try like mad to picture a pretty ocean with a setting sun. But then I remember that these "fish" may have come from that same ocean. So, I revert to the plan B of the psychologists: I assume a fetal position under my table.

I've always been a messy eater and the fish sticks have left a layer of grease on my fingers. It looks like I dipped my hands in a vat of Crisco for five days. When I ask the kid behind the counter if I can have some napkins, he tells me that they are only allowed to give out one per paying customer. This policy is used by all of the competing restaurants in the food court. And as such, the value of a napkin has increased exponentially. The United States used to base their entire economy upon something called "The Gold Standard." What we have now is a Food Court that bases all existence on something called "The Napkin Standard."

I somehow manage to eat half of the fish sticks on my plate. They were awful and tasted like used sponges. But I'm ready to move on. I discover that all five of the trash cans are filled to capacity, with impromptu towers of trash having been built by former customers. As there is no flat surface to place my plate on, I put my plate on the floor, hoping that nobody notices. Before leaving, I put my one sacred napkin on top of one of the leaning towers. This, of course, causes it to collapse and fall creating a loud ruckus. Instead of picking up all of the trash, I do the responsible thing and run away.

I later discover there is a reason that the mall directory signage is located so close to the food court. It is strategic. People who eat at the food court need to find the most direct route to the bathrooms. And fast. I'm no different. I just hope that the bathroom is cleaner than the food court.

CHAPTER SIX

The Audible Parasite

My experiment with the mall food court fish sticks left my stomach in ruins. After spending 20 minutes in the bathroom, I think it's safe to say that I won't be having a "silent night" this evening. But I won't let a little holiday explosion in my lower intestines ruin my chance at finding "The Christmas Spirit."

Speaking of "Silent Night", the song, not the Diarrhea-free slumber, that kind of music might be the thing I need to improve my outlook. I enjoy most of the traditional Christmas music. Bing Crosby's "White Christmas" and Nat King Cole's "The Christmas Song" are timeless classics that always seem to put me in the right mood during the holidays. It's unfortunate that what I currently hear coming over the mall's P.A. system puts me in the mood to begin dry heaving.

The song being played is called "Last Christmas." It was recorded by Wham!, the testosterone-deficient duo from the 80's. The band, having previously turned off fans of spilling secrets with its song, "Careless Whisper", then set its sights much higher with the goal of ruining a major holiday. I'll be honest; "Last Christmas" is 4 minutes and 34 seconds of pure holiday bunk. Ever since its release, scientists have been working feverishly to invent a time machine in order to reverse its harmful effects on the population.

Usually, when a band decides to record a song, they arrive at the recording session with the song's lyrics completed, or nearly so. In the case of "Last Christmas", the only thing George Michael brought to the session was a copy of "Mad Libs for Christmas Lyrics." His band mate, Andrew Ridgeley, presumably contributed something to the project as well, although precisely what has never been determined. Maybe he held the door open for the producers as they arrived.

1ST LYRIC:

"Last Christmas, I gave you my heart. But the very next day, you gave it away. This year, to save me from tears, I'll give it to someone special."

The Lyric's meaning?

It's one of the biggest myths in Christmas courtship. Guys make the mistake of believing that women appreciate it when they show their emotions. Not so. Note to George Michael: I think if "someone special" saw you crying like a little girl, they wouldn't think twice about throwing your heart away either. At the very least, they would throw away your phone number. Man up, for God's sake!

2ND LYRIC:

"Once bitten and twice shy. I keep my distance but you still catch my eye."

The Lyric's meaning? Sometimes, through time and tragedy, it's better to separate the artist from their work. I always enjoy looking at "The Starry Night" painting if I forget that Van Gogh later cut his ear off. An artist tortured by his inner demons. The same logic holds true for this lyric. The only reason George Michael "keeps his distance" is probably because he is under a restraining order after having exposed himself in a public bathroom. Demons.

3RD LYRIC:

"A crowded room, friends with tired eyes. I'm hiding from you and your soul of ice."

The Lyric's meaning? You've got me. I've read tax forms that were more engaging. Also, I was less concerned with the meaning of this line than with the fact that George tried to rhyme the word "eyes" with the word "ice." Did he really attempt that? If I had pulled that stunt in junior high English, my ass would have been flunked. I guess Wham! didn't have spell check available in 1984.

I can't really blame the mall for playing the song because it was included on a satellite-radio mix they subscribed to. Most likely, it was SiriusXM Radio Channel #217: "Songs That Are Slightly Less Annoying Than Monkey Sneezes"

Of course, disliking this song puts me in the minority as scores of other artists have covered the track. Still, I find it disturbing that most of the female covers offer voices that are lower in register than George Michael's version. Did someone kick him in his jingle bells before he recorded the tune?

As the song ends, the woman walking next to me starts to hum the song, thereby offering a free concert for those in ear-shot. Thanks lady. Now the dumb thing has attached itself to my brain like an audible parasite. I wish I had some different kinds of Christmas spirits to become inebriated.

Before I'm subjected to another song, I make my way over to a store that's quieter and offers "The Christmas Spirit" in spades: The Greeting Card Shop.

CHAPTER SEVEN

It's In The Cards

I'm thankful that Christmas cards still exist. Sometimes I think they are an endangered species. That's too bad. Now, it seems, everyone just sends a Facebook post with a silly lie about celebrating their "Greatest Christmas Ever!" Don't believe them. Like you, they also have unwanted items to return, insane in-laws to placate, and an annoying Christmas jingle they can't get out of their head. That's all normal. And greeting cards help to personalize such holiday struggle and indifference.

Before Christmas cards were invented, people had only a few options to convey Christmas cheer. If they had the means, they might have sent an expensive telegram. Or, if they were really feeling desperate, they may have resorted to actual conversation with their friend. In person. While making eye contact. Boy, I'm sure glad those days are behind us.

Compared to other holiday products, greeting cards have really evolved. The earliest Christmas cards wouldn't be recognizable next to the cards we know today. Those early versions probably included little more than a few lines of text and a picture on some sort of heavy card stock folded in half. My, how far we have come.

Today's modern card stores are highly organized places. And they make it easy to view the selections. What isn't as easy is deciding who to send the cards to. I used to divide my recipient list between "Close Family Members" and "Good Friends" but this seemed too vague. Eventually, I reached the same conclusion that so many of us reach at Christmas: "I sort of hate some of these people and a few of the others have been incarcerated." There has to be a better way of choosing.

So, exactly how do we know if they are worthy of a card? How can you measure true friendship at Christmas? Thankfully, I've invented a very simple system. It works like a charm and you're welcome to use it to build your own card lists. Basically, it includes two criteria: #1) You must be the kind of person who would drive me to the airport on only a few hours of notice. #2) If my flight should crash, you must also be willing to donate blood for my recovery. If you aren't A+ or a universal donor, I'm afraid you won't be getting a card this year. Tough but fair.

After your card list is created, you're ready to buy some Christmas cards. Today, people buy Christmas cards for a variety of reasons. It must be hard for the greeting card companies to market their product with so many different topics and themes. Of course, I could be over-thinking the challenge. For there are really only two motives I can think of that people have in sending a card. The first reason is that you and your loved ones are separated by a great distance and a card helps to bridge that distance with a declaration of love. The second reason is that you are, really, just a cheap S.O.B.

Don't forget that buying the card is just one part of the Christmas card process. You must also write a greeting on the inside. Sometimes I can't think of anything good to write. But even if you can't come up with the right words, there is help for you. The card companies employ expert writers who craft witty holiday sentiments. They are a talented bunch. Even on my best day, I couldn't come up with anything half as clever as these wordsmiths.

Months of intense brainstorming sessions yield impressive results for the card writers. Boring phrases like "Merry Christmas" and "I Love You" are transformed into beautiful prose. The new copy now reads, "Merry Christmas, Love!" and "I Love You, Mom!" You see, exclamation points and personal pronouns can be game changers in the greeting card industry. I guess that's why they are the "writers" and I'm just a non-writer, guy, person, thingy!

Although the writing help is nice, there are other advantages of buying Christmas cards. My favorite is the wide selection. The stores have a wide variety of cards for any holiday scenario. Like pets. The pet card genre has grown considerably over the years. For example, last Christmas I sent Tony, my personal trainer, a card that made light of his German Sheppard. Inside, the card text said, "I hope you and your bitch have a great Christmas!" It turned out that Tony didn't have a dog. But he did have a girlfriend. I guess that explains why I spent that Christmas in the hospital with two broken legs and major reconstructive surgery.

After all of your cards have been sent, you can expect two nice things to happen. First, each of your card recipients will feel a tremendous sense of appreciation toward you for having taken the time and effort to send them a card. And secondly, they will return the favor. Although the reciprocation comes in the form of a text message to your phone. It says, "THX! Lol!!!" If that doesn't pull at your heartstrings, nothing will. It's at that moment you realize that the card commercial didn't lie to you: "They cared just barely enough to send something really half-assed."

CHAPTER EIGHT

There Are Dumb Questions

One thing I really enjoy doing is people watching. This activity becomes even more enjoyable the closer I get to a shopping mall at Christmastime. The varied actions and appearances are striking. It's amazing what some people will do in public. Of course, seeing a man eat half of a Styrofoam plate at the food court has its limits. But overall, when I look at people from afar, it's great entertainment.

When I'm lucky enough to be close to these people, my people watching also includes people-listening. Some may find eavesdropping to be a nefarious act and that I should mind my own business. To those people, I simply say, this might be the most entertaining thing I do all month so cut me some slack.

Eavesdropping doesn't have to be looked down upon. After all, I am studying the human race. And I'm finding that loud apes often make more sense than people do. Here are the ten most overheard questions asked at the mall during Christmas season:

#1) "DO YOU WRAP GIFTS FOR FREE?"- The person who asks this question has just spent over $1,200 on several gifts. They'll be paying off credit card debt for months after Christmas. And just now they decide to be fiscally prudent with the free gift wrapping service? And let's be honest, the free wrapping service is nothing more than a legalized sweat shop for the department stores. Many sustain blisters and cuts on their fingers. Underage workers in Thailand probably have better working conditions than these underpaid wrappers. The good news for most of them is that if they wrap 100 gifts, they can take a bathroom break.

#2) "WHERE THE HELL IS MY CAR?"- I'm often guilty of losing my car in a large parking lot. And I feel like an idiot every time every time it happens. Spare change, I don't mind losing. But an entire car? I'm a college graduate for God's sake. When I can't find my car at the mall, it really bothers me. What bothers me more is that I know I'm just a few short years away from turning into one of those people who asks, "Where the Hell is the remote?", only to be answered with, "Umm, it's in your hand, Einstein."

#3) "HOW CAN I HELP YOU TODAY?"- Whenever I'm asked this by a salesperson, I always listen intently for which word of the question the seller places the most emphasis on. For example, "**HOW** can I help you today?" implies that they are out of ideas and need me to teach them how to operate a cash register. "How can **I** help you today?" leads me to believe that by me suggesting they know anything is laughable but that they would be happy to pass me off to another associate who also knows nothing. And finally, "How can I help you **TO-DAY**?" can mean only one thing: They are pissed that the store scheduled them for a Saturday afternoon and have no plans to make any effort until next week.

#4) "MY GOD, HAVE YOU EVER SEEN SO MANY IDIOTS IN ONE PLACE?"- Of course not. Malls at Christmastime are perfect breeding grounds for idiocy of the highest order. But even this mall doesn't hold the official record. On January 16, 1976, The Guinness Book of World Records recorded the highest level of pure idiocy at a mall in Pennsylvania. Out of 236 people who entered the mall, 203 of them attempted to Push when the doors were clearly marked, "Pull" On that day, the frigid temperature outside was actually higher than the collective I.Q. of the customers inside.

#5) "CAN I RETURN THIS WITHOUT A RECEIPT?"- If there's one thing that Christmas store employees love, it's when customers make their jobs more difficult. Still, I admire what some people are able to get away with when returning without a receipt. I think stores should assign a level of expertise for people using this tactic, depending on how successful they are. If you return a pair of socks without a receipt, you are considered a "Novice". If you return a flat screen T.V. to a gas station, you are labeled "Advanced" And if you are able to return your spouse to the Housewares department, congratulations, you are an "Expert" in the field.

#6) "DO YOU HAVE THIS IN A LARGER SIZE?"- After I turned 40, I noticed my pants started feeling more snug in the waist. This was, of course, odd. I had made the important decision a year earlier to limit my daily intake of Chips Ahoy cookies from 2 to 1. Mind you, that wasn't individual cookies but entire bags. The mirrors in the department store dressing room showed me that I needed to lose some weight. I had two options. I could either join a health club and work really hard for several months. Or, I could hold my breath indefinitely whenever I wore the new pants. The choice was obvious. I would wear the new pants for short, 30-second increments, and excuse myself to exhale.

#7) "CAN I SPEAK TO YOUR MANAGER?"- Somewhere around ten years ago, the phrase, "The Customer Is King" was changed to "The Customer Is An Indentured Servant and Should be Treated as Such." The switch caused some changes in many stores' customer service policies. Now, when you request to speak to a store manager, many stores simply roll out one of their store mannequins, lift up one of the arms, and then encourage you to talk directly into the fake hand. Get comfortable because a reply may take a while.

#8) "MOMMY, WHY ARE YOU CRYING?"- Let's see. Your mommy isn't crying because she is tired. She doesn't weep because the Christmas sale she read about ended two days ago. And she isn't sad because the lines are so long. Your mommy is crying because for the last 12 minutes, you, her precious angel, have been screaming at the top of your lungs about having to settle for a cookie with green frosting on it, as opposed to the one with red frosting. Kid, just be glad that you aren't asking her, "Mommy, why are you running away so fast?"

#9) "WOULD YOU LIKE TO TRY A FREE SAMPLE?"- Absolutely, I would! Oh wait, no I wouldn't because you are actually giving away things that are terrible. Saltines? Really? You can't entice me with something better than crackers during the important holiday season? Alright then, do you have the Saltines that have been dipped in chocolate? Do you make them with some sort of sweet, gooey substance in the center? I give up. Thankfully, I remember that it is better to give than receive. So I give my free sample right back to him.

#10) "HAVE YOU BEEN GOOD THIS YEAR?"– When I was a kid, sitting on Santa's lap, I always wished I would have taken the mall Santa to task, instead of having to answer this dumb question. It would have gone something like this, "What business is it of yours, fatso? Sure, I've done some questionable things this year, but how long must I carry this cross Santa? How Long!!?? Can't we all just get along?" Besides, "Good" is a relative term when its kids we are judging. I think if a kid can go the entire year without telling a fart joke, he deserves a new bike.

CHAPTER NINE

Attack Of The Ten-Foot Tree

I've just spent the past 3 hours in the Christmas Thunderdome, or "Shopping Mall", as it's officially known. And the inmates were clearly running the asylum. It feels good to leave the place. The fresh air feels liberating. The oxygen that was supposed to have occupied the mall's interior had long ago been consumed by blubbering fools screaming about the advantages of using store credit instead of cash. I just want to get home.

My escape plan takes a detour when I spot a Christmas tree seller at the edge of the parking lot. So I get out and take a look. What's the worst that can happen? I end up with a tree? No harm in that.

The tree lot itself is lit, barely, by 10-watt light bulbs attached to a sad looking string. This scene might put me in "The Christmas Spirit" had I spent the previous five years living in a dark cave in Afghanistan. I think more light could be displayed using old, flickering Revolutionary War-era lamps.

As this is two days before Christmas, all of the good trees are, of course, gone. What's left are the losers of the tree world. The pathetic, last trees chosen, much like the uncoordinated kids who had the audacity to want to play kickball on the playground. I can hear other people voice their displeasure, "Leave my sight, skinny one! How dare you call yourself a Christmas Tree!"

I've never been one to take part in the whole "Real Vs. Fake" argument that you always hear concerning Christmas trees. It seems pointless. If you like natural, then fine. If you like fake, knock yourself out. It doesn't matter much to me. To me, the only "Real Vs. Fake" argument worth participating in is the one that attempts to discern the authenticity of Halle Barry's, umm, ornaments.

What am I doing here? I've no idea how I'll be able to transport any tree in my small car. With 4 bags of merchandise already in the trunk, there won't be any room left. The owner says it won't be a problem as he has the ability to tie the tree to the roof of my car. The owner is also missing three teeth and I wonder why he couldn't have tied those down using the same method.

Christmas tree lot owners are just a few steps away from being carnival operators, or "Carnies." In fact, many got their start fleecing people in un-winnable carnival games. Carnies don't like to lose. Carnies also hate it when customers leave their booth with a large item, like a stuffed animal. Conversely, Christmas tree sellers love it when a sucker like me leaves with a large item, like a tree with a stump that's bent in 5 places.

Basically, I have two choices: A small, ugly tree, with half its needles missing. Or a giant, ten foot tree that looks amazing from all angles. I choose the healthy giant and believe I've just found the greatest deal in the history of commerce. Only the Louisiana Purchase was a better bargain.

The tree comes with a stand. But this stand, manufactured with tin, isn't up to the task. It was made in Guatemala and probably couldn't prop up a potted plant if it had to. Maybe a single, solitary sunflower. I could go out and get a better stand. But since I'm stubborn, I'll do just about anything to prop it up using desperate techniques, as is the Christmas tradition.

There have been many great "proppings" in the history of the United States. When our engineers built Hoover Dam, we saw how technology could prop up water to create energy. When the soldiers propped up the American flag at Iwo Jima, it became a symbol for our ingenuity and perseverance. But tonight, the attempt at propping up my tree is developing into a symbol for my special brand of laziness. Damn. I could have used those engineers.

Because my tree's stump is bent in five different places, it won't matter how strong the stand is. I need major help. Structural engineers will tell you that if you don't have a good, strong, solid base, it won't matter what you are attempting to build. I agree. This is why I'm placing it on stacks of old, crumpled up newspaper.

My secret weapon in this endeavor is the hard cover Encyclopedia Britannica, volume "F". I immediately place it under the rear leg of the stand to combat the noticeable lean. I'm not sure what is more sad: the fact that I'm using books to prop up the tree or the fact that I own encyclopedias. The "F" volume is appropriate, however. The "F" stands for "Fiasco" and "Falling."

After all of my construction ideas are implemented, the tree leans noticeably to the left. I'm tempted to cut a hole through my ceiling, hire professional marionette operators, and have them hold up the tree with string as they make the tree dance during the day. Thankfully, I come to my senses and make a much more appropriate decision: I just won't approach the tree within a 50-foot diameter. And this will go on until after Christmas.

Since I bought this dumb tree, it means that I have to somehow decorate it. I own no ornaments. And the only lights in my possession are a short strand, with half of them burned out. Also, I have no decorating experience. Men don't decorate. That's not entirely true. When I was a kid, I worked in a grocery store bakery. A woman once asked me to decorate a birthday cake for her daughter. When I completed the decorating, it looked like a toddler had written the words using finger paint. Maybe I won't decorate my tree and just say that I like the "natural" look.

The next morning, I wake up to find the tree is still leaning. And the lean has become more pronounced. Eventually, it falls over as if Paul Bunyan himself chopped it down, gleefully. And the only question going through my mind is, "Can I return this without a receipt?"

There's no returning a Christmas tree! So, I shove the tree into a corner and find that that works for me at the moment. I need to run an errand, anyway. Maybe the tree will teach itself to walk and stand upright on its own while I'm gone.

There is but one item left on my to-do list. I need to mail some boxes filled with Christmas presents at the Post Office. As I've gotten up super early, I anticipate a seamless, enjoyable experience where "The Christmas

Spirit" will be evident all over the place at the govern-
ment-run facility.

CHAPTER TEN

Going Postal

Getting up early seems to be a recurring theme that runs throughout the Christmas season. The crazy Black Friday shoppers got up early so they could buy stuff they'll never use. Little kids get up early on Christmas morning to survey their haul from the North Pole. And then there's me. Today, I'm getting up early to stand in line at the Post Office. It's beginning to look a lot like a Circus.

I set my alarm for 6:00am. This is a few hours earlier than I wanted to wake up. But I knew that if I was to mail my Christmas gifts before the other yahoos, I would need to be at the post office right when they opened their doors. I figured that two hours would be plenty to get my tired butt there on time. It turns out that half of the city had the same idea as me. So much for waking up early.

Before I even set foot in the building I accept certain truths. Some things in life are inevitable. Death. Taxes. And slow postal workers. This isn't a new discovery. And most people know that long lines are a permanent feature at the post office. What they may not have realized are the rate increases. I'm not sure but I think if you put a bow on your package, it'll cost you an extra $70.00 to send it these days.

I guess I wouldn't mind spending time at the place if it were just a little more welcoming. From my experience, most postal workers look as if they've just awoken from major surgery. And not a fun surgery like Lasik, either. But an invasive procedure like an Appendectomy that rattles you to the core. They're a little dazed and confused. And they'll be the first to let you know that you're not welcome past visiting hours.

Reality has set in for the Postal Service at Christmas. Budgets have been cut. I'm sure that having insufficient funds to operate their business must be sobering. Reality comes in other forms at the post office, too. Mainly that the Postmaster General is not a dynamic superhero who can use his secret powers to clone more postal workers. That won't be possible until the second-half of this century.

So then, what *can* we do? Some people say that post office workers need a fire lit under their ass. That's kind of harsh, don't you think? Instead, we should light small firecrackers under their toes to encourage speedy movement. And it would help to update their old slogan: "Neither snow, nor rain, nor strategically placed Roman Candles can prevent us from delivering your mail this Christmas."

I shouldn't complain. I think those who only complain are a part of the problem. So, instead, I'd like to offer some ideas on how the post office can improve their image during Christmas. If the biggest problem is long lines, entertain us! We know we can't ever change the wait times. That idea is a pipe dream. So let's concentrate on the user experience while we wait.

If you're stuck waiting for longer than 10 minutes, the post office should let you answer a kid's "Dear Santa" letter in any style or tone you wish. Here's what mine would say, "Dear Christopher: I received your nice letter last week. Yes, I am real. I do exist. And I'm doing just fine. So you can rest easy. However, we had Rudolph stuffed this year because he was getting too lippy with the other reindeer. Warmest regards, Santa Claus."

If your wait exceeds 20 minutes, I think you should be allowed to purchase baseballs for a "Dunk The Letter Carrier" game. Who wouldn't like to see their mailman dropped in cold water? And assuming that the carrier is sane, you wouldn't have to worry about them "Going Postal" this Christmas.

If for some reason your wait should go over the agonizing 30 minute mark, congratulations! You are now qualified to sit in the co-pilot seat of the United States Postal Service's premier delivery vehicle as they make a delivery! Unfortunately, the most advanced delivery vehicles they operate are donkey carts and Hydrogen-inflated Zeppelins. Have fun.

The woman in front of me has decided to purchase special holiday stamps from the man at the counter. The stamps have a simple message on them that says, "LOVE". That's cute. What isn't as cute is the permanent scowl on the post office employee's face. If the post office really wanted to give people a sense of what an actual day is like at their organization, they should release new holiday stamp sets that say, "APATHY" and "INDIFFERENCE".

I get the sense that my bad attitude will come back to haunt me here at the post office. Christmas Karma is even more severely dealt out than regular Karma. Certainly much more than Halloween Karma. And I haven't exactly given my post office workers the benefit of the doubt. But my packages have been stamped, metered, and directed to the next stage. Everything seems to have gone more smoothly than I anticipated. Maybe I got lucky?

As I make my way outside, one of the postal workers actually smiles at me and says, "Have a great Christmas!"

Stunned, I return the greeting and wish him well. At that point, I begin to feel what others have described to me as "The Christmas Spirit." It's pure. It really does exist. And it feels pretty good.

And then it happens. I take a shortcut through the grass toward my car. When I get within ten feet of it, I step in something soft and slippery. A giant pile of dog poop. Steamy. Recent. And judging by the size, it could have been deposited by a horse.

"The Christmas Spirit" exists everywhere and in different ways. My friend would be proud. Looks like I've finally put myself in it.

Dear Reader:

Thanks very much for taking the time to read "Christmas Mall Follies." Please consider leaving a review at www.amazon.com. Also, if you would like to receive information on my next book, please visit www.pathester.com.

Regards,
Pat Hester